MW01610491

How To Lose Weight With Magic Spells.

Contents:

4) Hoodoo diet spell

5) Banish a bad habit charm

6) Weight loss aid

7) Fitness spell

8) Beautiful body potion

9) Mirror weight loss spell

10) Shrink my waist spell

11) Slimming spell

12) Slim me down

13) Will power

14) Run faster

15) Younger spell

16) To help the weight loss of a friend

17) Another simple diet spell

18) Weight loss magic

19) Cookies that give you power

20) Muscle growth spell

21) Skinny

22) 20 pounds down!

23) Extremely powerful weightloss spell

1) Simple Diet Spell

Baking-soda

Salt

Blood

Bowl

Water

First you will need to fill a bowl with water

Then take a drop blood in the water. Continue with filling the bowl with a spoon of salt and at the end put just a little baking-soda and then say...

I drink of My own blood to make me lose weight

...Then drink it 5 Times if you want to lose 5 kiloes and if you want to lose more then drink more but when you are finished with drinking you need to say...

So mote it be!

...You wont feel hungry after this, but after Mabye two hours you will

WARNING: It can taste discusting and U will feel a little weird at the stomach

2) Diet Potion

Plain white 7 day advent candle (The kind in a tall glass holder)
Picture of yourself at current weight
Rubber bands or string

Start this spell on the 3 day after the Full Moon. If possible at the start of the week (Sunday, Monday or Tuesday). Hold the candle in you hands and as you charge it with energy to help you loose weight say the following 3x:

"With the waning of the moon this spell I now begin; To help me loose weight and back in shape I wish to be in. As this candle melts away, So I will loose weight each day. With the help of the gods a myself I demand pounds to melt away and bring me better health."

Now place the candle down and take up the picture of yourself. Concentrate on the picture for a good minute. Then close your eyes and visualize the image of you slowly shrinking in size, till you wish to get to that desired weight and look. When done take the picture and warp it about the candle jar. Use rubber bands or cord to hold it against the jar. Now light the candle. And as you do say the following"

"I wish to lose weight I don?t need This spell will help me to succeed I?ll exercise, eat healthy food I?ll be resolved in mind and mood I?ll be more healthy, this I vow I?ll work to lose weight, starting now"

Let the candle burn during your workout and one hour after that. Then extinguish it. Repeat this spell everyday till the candle is burned out.

3) Energy Potion

alfalfa leaves

ginkgo biloba leaves

coffee filter.

grind alfalfa leaves and ginkgo biloba leaves in a bowl.

when done grinding, place into small pot or cauldron and add water

boil the leaves for 2 minutes, or until water color changes.

when done boiling. put filter over cup and pour contents of the pot into the

cup.

if you want, you may add sugar or any sweetener for taste.

4) Hoodoo Diet Spell

rosemary

Aphrodite statue

red candle

yellow candle

pink candle

purple candle

gold candle

lip stick

paper

markers

attraction oil

Venus incense

On a piece of paper with markers draw a picture of yourself and your full body of how you want your body to look like. Use markers to create this picture as legit as you can also after, outline your body with the color of your aura. After you draw yourself how you want to look, write your goal weight number and affirmation words to help manifest your desire such as motivation, determination, ambition, success, victory, beautiful, goals, aspirations, fit, healthy, etc. Be sure to also write your full name above the image you drew of yourself. Then, place the drawing on your alter. In the center of your drawing place a gold candle and color the rim of the candle with the lipstick. Anoint the gold candle with attraction oil. Then in front of the gold candle place the yellow candle to represent burning your fat away.

Behind the gold candle place Aphrodite's statue and behind her the red candle. On the left side of Aphrodite place the pink candle and on Aphrodite's right side place the purple candle. Then, sprinkle rosemary on the picture you drew and in the candles. Allow the candles to sit and burn for 20-30 minutes. After that time is up burn Venus incense. Focus on your intention and strong will towards the body that you desire. Chant.....

"Aphrodite oh Venus of mine I call to thee during the witching hour divine.

I ask of thee oh goddess of love and beauty to manifest the body that I desire.

I light this gold candle to represent your divine energy, red for strength and passion, pink for your love, purple for healing, and yellow to resemble burning my fat away.

Oh dear Goddess Aphrodite this is my plea I ask of thee make me beautiful, healthy, and as fit as can be.

Help me lose weight and with this yellow candle I now burn and melt my fat away.

I thank thee goddess for your divine energy and presence in helping me to achieve my bodies potential and desire to be so mote it be!"

.....Wait for your incense to burn completely out and then it is complete.

5) Banish a bad habit charm

Paper

A pen or pencil

A candle (I have one of those candles that's in a glass. You Might want to use one of those)

A glass

A glass of water

A Lighter

Write your bad habit on a piece of paper.

For example eating too many unhealthy things.

Light the candle... The candle needs to be in a glass... Then burn the paper.

Scold to it as if it's a person you are really angry at... Say your bad habit out loud. "I WILL NOT EAT UNHEALTHY THINGS"

Pour the glass of water onto the candle... the paper and the wax is now kind of melted together. Take the ashes and fold it into another piece of paper. You can decorate it if you want to. I used a candywrap instead of folding it into normal paper.

Keep it with you as a charm to remind you not to do something.

6) Weight loss aid

1 Clear Quartz Crystal

1 Green Candle

1 Green Draw-String Bag

BEST DONE: outside, or by an open window, on a clear night, 3 days after the full moon

Cast the circle. Sit and meditate, concentrating on all the positive that will come from loosing weight [health, strength, new wardrobe, looks] when ready, light the green candle and hold the crystal in dominant [writing] hand, say:

Goddess within,

Goddess without.

Guide me to my goal.

Ease my hunger,

Sooth my spirit,

Strengthen my resolve

As I will it, So Mote it Be!

Raising the crystal over your head concentrate now on all the negative aspects of dieting. [cravings, temptations, cheating, hard work] Draw all negative thoughts into the crystal, continue until the candle burns out. [or snuff out candle when ready] Leave the crystal in the windowsill in the moonlight overnight.

In the morning, place the crystal in the green pouch and carry it on you.

7) Fitness spell

Visualize a white gold energy in and around yourself.

Now hold this visualization, only this time visualize yourself as physically fit.

Hold this visualization while affirming "I am physically fit". Affirm 5-10 times. Be sure to do this on a regular basis for results.

8) Beautiful body potion

Blue Candle

Red Candle

Black Candle

Silver Candle

Garcinia Combogia Extract

Water

Small bowl or normal size cup

Salt (optional if you use pepper)

Pepper (optional if you use salt)

Take your extract, water, salt and / or pepper, and mix them in equal porportions (everything except the water) and mix it in your cup/bowl.

Spell:

Make your potion, and place the cup / bowl with the finished product in from of you. Now pretend the bowl / cup is a square. Put two candles on the right and left upper "corners" and the last candle on the upper "side" and light each of them.

Then chant:

"Earth grown herbs, witches brew, Soon the weight I am now will the weight I once knew. Help me lose weight, This is my will."

Blow the candles out. Take a sip of the potion. Everyday exercise for 30 minutes, then take a sip of the potion, do this until the potion is all gone.

9) Mirror weight loss spell

Meditate during the waning moon.

Light a pink candle for self-love.

Anoint it with the oil of your choice.

Next light a brown candle, engrave the number of pounds you want to loose on it. Then visualize banishing the excess weight.

Runes can also be carved on the candle if you wish and incense can be burned.

Visualize the smoke taking the excess pounds away!

10) Shrink my waist spell

White and orange candles

Measuring tape

Sticky Tape

White or orange cord

Paper

Pen

Permanent marker

Heat safe plate

Waning moon

Light the candles.

Write on one side of the paper what your current waist measurement is, then on the other side write what you wish it to be.

Place the paper, current side up, in front of the candles.

Mark on the measuring tape where you wish your waist to measure with the adhesive tape, then x out where you are now with the permanent marker.

Sit and meditate. Visualize how you will look and feel when you are at your goal. Really feel the pride, happiness, excitement, etc.

Once you have a solid picture of it all in your mind, take the paper and burn each end in the flame of one of the candles and place on the plate, imagining that the inches are burning away with the paper.

Take the cord and begin to tie knots, starting at one end and alternating while moving from the outside inward until you reach 9 knots.

Now tie it around your wrist.

By this time the paper should be ash, so gather the ash and release it into the winds, saying...

"so mote it be"

...as the ashes float away.

As your waist shrinks, mark off the new measurement with the marker until you hit the tape.

Once you reach your goal, bury the cord as an offering to the earth.

11) Slimming spell

1 big/long white candle

Lighter

Light the candle with your lighter , close your eyes and say...

"O ignis spiritus, adiuva me tollendum adipem de me, et libera me mundane

novae figurae, precor te, ut me adiuvet amittere pondus o judices"

...Stand their until you feel wax pouring down your hands, it might hurt a bit,

but stay focused and imagine the pouring wax as your fat and chubbiness

pouring and melting.

12) Slim me down!

Consentration

White candle (optional)

Picture of the castee (optional)

Belief

Begin by meditating for 10-15 minutes prior to casting.

Light the candle and concentrate on the flame. Imagine your subject (or yourself) as light as the flame, weightless even. Do this for 5 minutes.

Now the picture is to be used if you can't accuratly visulize the person, but if you are able to you have no need for it. Visulize the subject and keep them as the focal point as your thoughts imagine them on a scale and the scales number is slowly dropping. How long u do this is all up to you.

Say this chant according to the amount of weight you wish to be lost. For instance, 30 pounds you say it 3 times so on so forth...

This is the chant...

"I ask of thee to help a friend (or yourself) to lose unwanted weight. What they may loose in body weight may they gain in happiness. I ask of thee to assist"

...After your last chant end with so mote it be.

13) Will power

candle (large and light blue)

candle (long and white)

candle (small and purple)

potpourri (any type)

matches

incense (any type)

This is a meditation spell. You will require a number of candles. Basically any shape candles but their colors should be light blue, white or purple.

This spell can be cast anywhere where you can remain for a period of time (the longer the better) and where you will be undisturbed and comfortable. Light the candles and start the incents or potpourri (you don?t need both, just one, or if the candles are scented that works as well).

Lay down in your comfortable place and chant the following chant...

"Give me strength and guide me right,

To my goals when they?re in sight,

But even when they?re far away;

Guide myself towards the day

When I shall stand upon the shore

My conflicts gone forever more.

And guide myself to make the choice,

That I can?t bring myself to voice;

And calm my tormented, ravaged soul,

From right now till forever more."

...The more often the chant is spoken, the more will power you will be given. The spell will fade over time and it is best if it is cast weekly

14) Run faster

Go out on the nice sunny day.

Meditate.

Close eyes.

While eyes are closed, chant 3 times...

"God of speed, allow me to run fast ,but not be seen"

15) Younger spell

water

a hair from 3 year old

a scab

First put the scab and hair in water.

Put your hand in the water and close your eyes chant this twice...

"I wish to be younger.

I wish to be (how old you want to be). Hagina kaykay!"

...Side affects: Acting like a kid, Eating mustard, getting in trouble

16) To help the weight loss of a friend

Candle (any color)

Saucer (for the candle)

paper

pen

match or lighter

Place the candle on the saucer and set it down.

Sit down before the candle and light it.

Tear the paper in half (hamburger style) and write the person's name down in the middle.

Hold the paper with the name on it over the flame.

As it burns, say this chant...

"20, 30, 40 pounds off,

Help this person lose weight,

Let it be as fast as a cough,

And for his [or her] health to be great.

This is my will, so mote it be."

17) Another simple diet spell

1 yellow candle

1 knife

This spell should be performed during a waxing moon on a night on which you can see the moon.

It should be performed outside or with an open window facing the moon.

Take the candle and point it to the sky.

Imagine yourself thin.

Carve the wish into the candle.

Light it while saying...

"Tonight I come to you young Moon,

help my efforts to not be in vain

help me now to lose my burden,

may I lose so you may gain."

...Let the candle burn down then throw it away.

18) Weight Loss Magic!

A pink candle

A yellow candle

Jasmine incense

Olive oil

This spell should be performed during the waning phase of the moon.

Firstly, anoint the candles with the olive oil... Start with the white candle and then the yellow... The pink candle should be anointed at the end.... Begin to coat the oil starting at the bottom and going downwards all the way in one go.

Coat all the candles in this fashion. Decide on how many pounds of weight you want to shed and divide it by three. Carve the number on each candle. If you want to lose fifteen pounds, you need to carve out the number 5 on each of the candles. If it is an odd number divide the number in such a way that each candle has only very slight variation.

Once this is done, set up an altar on a flat surface. Light the white candle and place it at the center. To the left of the white candle, place the yellow one and to the right of the white candle, place the pink one. Cast a circle around the candles and light the incense. Jasmine incense can be used for women and Patchouli incense can be used for men. Then light the candles and meditate upon them. Visualize that you are having the excess weight banished from your body.

Have another glass cup inserted with a wick. As the white, yellow and pink candles burn, pour out the wax into this cup. In this way you will be able to make a new candle. Burn this new candle everyday until you lose the desired number of pounds

19) Cookies that give you power

2 3/4 cups all-purpose flour

1 teaspoon baking soda

1/2 teaspoon baking powder

1 cup softened butter

1 1/2 cups white sugar

1 egg

1 teaspoon vanilla extract

4 to 5 tablespoons buttermilk

1 tablespoon coffe

2 crushed anise seeds

Preheat oven to 375 degrees F.

In a small bowl, stir together flour, baking soda, coffe, baking powder. Set this aside.

In a large bowl, cream together butter and sugar until smooth. Beat in the egg and vanilla. Gradually blend in dry ingredients. Add enough of the buttermilk to moisten the dough and make it soft, not wet.

Roll rounded teaspoons of dough into balls and place on a ungreased cookie sheet. With a brush or fingers, moisten the top of each cookie with the remaining buttermilk and slightly flatten the top of each cookie. Sprinkle with raw sugar or colored sprinkles.

Bake for 8 to 10 minutes, or until slightly golden. Let stand for 2 minutes before removing to cool on a rack.

20) Muscle growth spell

1 red candle

1 white candle

1 picture of what you wish to look like

1 fire (NOT THE FIRE FROM THE CANDLES A SEPERATE FIRE)

Place the red candles on your left and the white candle on your right. hold the picture tightly to you close your eyes and with total concentration say...

"To look like this is my wish,

make my body change,

for i am not happy with who i may be."

...Now burn the picture. and chant again while the picture is burning

21) Skinny

↗

Go to a mirror.

Touch it and say...

"I wish to be weightless,

my thighs will be slim,

I want to be __ pounds,

thin body, thin limbs.

my stomach will be flat,

no matter what I eat,

my hip bones will show,

they're easy to see,

this is my will,

so mote it be."

...Say this FIVE TIMES. Then kiss the mirror

22) 20 pounds down!

Energy Drink
Cupcake

Put the energy in front of the cupcake and say..

Upon These Days I'm so fat that,

I couldn't rage I wish to be,

A Exercising Beast,

if I loose the 20 Pounds,

I need to see,

I'll take care of your wife earth,

uranus, Venus I'll make you popular,

also I call upon the spirits to message your love ones,

if you do this,

please for sake,

this is my will,

so Mote it be.

23)Extremely powerful weightloss spell

1 red candle

1 orange candle

1 yellow candle

1 green candle

1 blue candle

1 indigo candle

1 violet candle

1 white candle

1 black candle

1 blossom from a bleeding heart flower

red ribbon

matches

red pen

paper

crystal bowl

Set the nine candles up in a circle, with the white and black candles opposite each other.

The circle must be big enough for you to sit cross-legged in.

Lay a red ribbon on the floor, connecting the white and black candles.

Light the candles.

With the red pen, write the following on the piece of paper...

I wish to lose weight

wish to lose weight

ish to lose weight

sh to lose weight

h to lose weight

to lose weight

o lose weight

lose weight

ose weight

se weight

e weight

weight

eight

ight

ght

ht

t

Pass the paper through the flames of each of the candles once, burning it, but not setting it on fire.

Put the paper in the crystal bowl.

Light each end of the ribbon on fire, one with the white candle, one with the black candle.

Put the ribbon in the bowl.

Once the fire has died down, go outside, and blow the ashes into the wind, imagining yourself losing ten pounds and looking beautiful.

Repeat the spell for every extra ten pounds you eant to lose... So, if you want to lose fifty pounds, do the spell five times.

Manufactured by Amazon.ca
Bolton, ON

33410177R00022